The Constitution Minute

♦

A Series of Commentaries on the Constitutional Issues of the Day

Randall Yearout

Edited by Karen Murray

Red, White & Blue Collar Radio

Cover design: Matthew Murray, Animator-Designer-Developer, ww.mattmurrayanimation.com

Front cover photo: *Scene at the Signing of the Declaration of Independence*, Howard Chandler Christy

Letterwriting, Pen, and Ink; www.fromoldbooks.org. Public domain.
Yearout Family: Ruddell Photography of Spokane, Washington
Randall Yearout Campaign Portrait: Robert W. Peck of Spokane Valley, Washington
Randall At Work: Robert W. Peck of Spokane Valley, Washington
The Birth of Old Glory, **Moran:** Library of Congress, Prints & Photographs Division, [reproduction number, LC-USZC4-2791]; public domain.
Molly Pitcher, **engraving, 1859:** public domain.
Destruction of Tea at Boston Harbor, Lithograph by Currier & Ives: public domain.
Nathan Hale Hanged by the British, 1776: www.ushistoryimages.com
Paul Revere's Midnight Ride: public domain.

© 2011 Red, White & Blue Collar Radio. All Rights Reserved.
ISBN: 978-1-4583-4283-6

**Dedicated to the Liberty of our Children
who must live with
the Consequences of our Actions.**

CONTENTS

Preface – 5

Who is Randall Yearout? - 7

Jurisdiction – 9

Natural Law - 11

Virtue - 13

Leaders - 15

Common Law - 17

The Creed - 19

Civil Authority and Scripture - 21

Principle vs. Politics - 23

Subversion - 25

Crime and Rights - 27

Religion and Morality - 29

Oath of Office - 31

Jury Nullification - 33

Treaties and Sovereignty - 35

General Welfare - 37

The Creator - 39

A Constitutionist's Proposal for Restoring the American Republic - 41

About the Constitution Party – 51

The Yearout Family

Preface

"This is Randall Yearout on..."

So begin the Constitution Minute radio spots, which began playing on the American Christian Network radio system across eastern Washington, north Idaho, and northeast Oregon in the summer of 2009. Since then the Constitution Minute has made it to the west coast of Washington, as well as several other states.

I first met Randall in 2008, during the presidential campaign of Chuck Baldwin who was running on the Constitution Party ticket. He spoke at the rally held in Spokane and I was impressed with his knowledge of constitutional principles and his blue collar manner of explaining them so all could clearly understand their meaning.

It is what America needs now, a clear understanding of those principles upon which this nation, unlike any other nation, was founded. In the 1960's a popular saying went like this, "As GM goes, so goes the nation." Today, "As America goes, so goes the world." If America moves back towards the roots of liberty, then the world will follow. If America continues to slide into the New World Order, the world will be ruled by economic despots bent on controlling global resources, global manpower, and global societies in an effort to "save Humanity from itself." The loss of American principles means the loss of liberty for everyone.

We need more men like Randall Yearout who have awakened to an awful sense of our predicament as a nation and as a people. More men to educate themselves, as Randall has done. More men to stand up and be counted as Randall has done – as a husband and father, as an educator of constitutional principles, as a sought after speaker at political events, and twice as a candidate for United State House of Representatives.

Randall is a blue collar worker. He is a crane operator and skilled saddle maker. This is the grassroots of America and it is men such as this who will stand up and say "Not on my watch." They will stand with pitchfork and computer, microphone and crane, internet and tractor, rifle and pickup truck, in the same manner as our ideological and physical ancestors did when Divine Providence called them to participate in the first American Revolution. This is our generation's "rendezvous with destiny". Where will you be?

As for me I am proud to be a member of the "vast American-wing conspiracy" as Randall so astutely puts it in the signature closing line of each Constitution Minute—

"This is a pair of Constitution minutes with Randall Yearout at Red, White & Blue Collar Radio, brought to you by the vast American-wing conspiracy at the Constitution Party of Washington. Contact them at constitutionpartyofwa.com"

Karen Murray, Editor
12 February 2011

Randall Yearout at Work

Who is Randall Yearout?

Randall Yearout is a statesman, dedicated to educating his family, friends, neighbors and the citizenry of these united States on the authority of our Constitution.

Randall and his wife, Holly, as of 2011 will have been married 30 years. Together they raised and homeschooled 3 now-grown children and are blessed with 8 grandchildren. They live on a small rural property in Newman Lake, Washington.

Since 1978 he has been a member in good standing with the International Union of Operating Engineers and operated heavy equipment for both private contractors and at the Hanford nuclear reservation. Randall moved his family from the Tri-Cities to Spokane in 1995 after an injury that left him disabled, where he attended the Saddle Making School at Spokane Falls Community College, after which he opened and operated his own saddle shop. Since then, he has returned to the building trades as a crane operator for a locally owned small business.

Studying our founders and educating himself on the Constitution and its principles has been a passion to which Randall has dedicated the past 10 years. He has instructed "The Institute on the Constitution" numerous times as well as helping to oversee the Constitution Party's monthly Continuing Education classes. Randall is writing and producing the "Constitution Minute" which is aired on radio stations regionally as well as being utilized by other state Constitution Party affiliates coast to coast.

He and his wife are both national delegates for the Constitution Party. Randall was the Constitution party's candidate for the 5th Congressional District U.S. House seat in the 2008 election, securing an admirable number of votes as an unknown running on a 3rd party ticket.

UNITED STATES CONSTITUTION, Article 4, Section 3:
"The Congress shall have Power to dispose of and make all needful Rules and Regulations respecting the Territory or other Property belonging to the United States; and nothing in this Constitution shall be so construed as to Prejudice any Claims of the United States, or of any particular State."

UNITED STATES CONSTITUTION, NINTH AMENDMENT
"The enumeration in the Constitution, of certain rights, shall not be construed to deny or disparage others retained by the people."

TENTH AMENDMENT
"The powers not delegated to the United States by the Constitution, nor prohibited by it to the States, are reserved to the States respectively, or to the people."

CONSTITUTION PARTY PLATFORM
- ★ The federal republic was created by joint action of the several states.
- ★ It has been gradually perverted into a socialist machine for federal control in the domestic affairs of the states.
- ★ The federal government has no authority to mandate policies relating to state education, natural resources, transportation, private business, housing, healthcare, ad infinitum.
- ★ We call upon the states to reclaim their legitimate role in federal affairs and legislation, thus causing the federal government to divest itself of operations not authorized by the Constitution and extract the federal government from such enterprises, whether or not they compete with private enterprises.

Jurisdiction

When the U. S. territories applied for admission into the Union as states, the overarching principle that drove this decision was the desire for sovereignty to determine their own destinies, and to be removed from what the U.S. Constitution calls the *"exclusive legislative jurisdiction"* of the Congress over the properties owned by the U.S. government. The state of Washington removed itself from this *"exclusive jurisdiction"* in 1889, and was required to write its own Constitution, which would provide for a representative republican form of government for its citizens. Such is the case for every state which joined our Union.

Today, our U.S. government officials and bureaucrats have lost sight of this fact, and now want to re-assert *"exclusive legislative jurisdiction"* over the states, turning them into administrative subdivisions, as though we were territories again. Sorry, U.S. government, but the Constitution says you don't have that authority; and Americans are beginning to realize that our founders intended for the individual states to either succeed or fail based on their own laws and policies. If the people don't like the way a particular state operates, they can move to another one where they do. The way our federal government operates today, the entire nation either succeeds or fails based on the policies of 535 legislators in Washington, D.C.; and from what we can see from its history of failed social policies, I don't think these guys could pour sand out of their boots if the directions were written on the heel.

We need to replace the socialist mindset in Washington D.C., and our state governments, with a restored American view of law and government.

Declaration of Independence, 4 July 1776

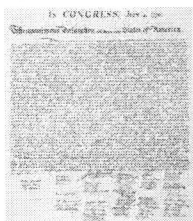

"When in the Course of human events, it becomes necessary for one people to dissolve the political bands which have connected them with another, and to assume among the powers of the earth, the separate and equal station to which the Laws of Nature and of Nature's God entitle them, a decent respect to the opinions of mankind requires that they should declare the causes which impel them to the separation.

We hold these truths to be self-evident, that all men are created equal, that they are endowed by their Creator with certain unalienable Rights, that among these are Life, Liberty and the pursuit of Happiness. That to secure these rights, Governments are instituted among Men, deriving their just powers from the consent of the governed, That whenever any Form of Government becomes destructive of these ends, it is the Right of the People to alter or to abolish it, and to institute new Government, laying its foundation on such principles and organizing its powers in such form, as to them shall seem most likely to effect their Safety and Happiness. Prudence, indeed, will dictate that Governments long established should not be changed for light and transient causes; and accordingly all experience hath shewn, that mankind are more disposed to suffer, while evils are sufferable, than to right themselves by abolishing the forms to which they are accustomed. But when a long train of abuses and usurpations, pursuing invariably the same Object evinces a design to reduce them under absolute Despotism, it is their right, it is their duty, to throw off such Government, and to provide new Guards for their future security."

Natural Law

As Americans, and especially as Christians, we have great need to understand a concept that our founding fathers counted as the most important principle of all; and they expected their descendants and their leaders never to lose sight of it. It is the principle of regard for the *"laws of nature and nature's God"*. It is of first prominence in the Declaration of Independence. Our Constitution, national greatness and blessing are a product of this understanding. Private and civil institutions, government, schools and families used to be fervent in their application of this principle, and as a result, America has been God-blessed almost beyond the comprehension of most of the rest of the world.

Today, however, most of our leaders come from law schools or universities where the *"laws of nature and nature's God"* are ridiculed and mocked. The U.S. Constitution is either explained away as irrelevant or ignored altogether. We have ceded control of our schools and government to men whose purpose-whose religion- is to create a world in their own image. Their goal is within sight, and we are beginning to experience the introduction to this new world order in the form of our national decline.

American freedom and individual liberty are the main objectives of our American form of law and government, but as you can clearly see today, that objective doesn't have a place to stand in a government which ignores and ridicules God's law. Proverbs 22:28 tells us *"Remove not the ancient landmark which thy fathers have set."* Our president and on down seem to be bent on doing just that, and the removal of national blessing is being realized on our watch.

George Washington's Farewell Address, 17 September 1796

"Of all the dispositions and habits which lead to political prosperity, **Religion and Morality** are indispensable supports. In vain would that man claim the tribute of Patriotism, who should labor to subvert these great pillars of human happiness, these firmest props of the duties of Men and Citizens. The mere Politician, equally with the pious man, ought to respect and to cherish them. A volume could not trace all their connections with private and public felicity...And let us with caution indulge the supposition that morality can be maintained without religion. Whatever may be conceded to the influence of refined education on minds of peculiar structure, reason and experience both forbid us to expect that national morality can prevail in exclusion of religious principle."

Williamstown Portrait of George Washington
Artist, Gilbert Stuart

Virtue

In the years just preceding our American War for Independence, there was a popular concern with whether we were a virtuous enough people to be able to govern ourselves. In other words, could we live as a people, a nation in a way which would bring God's blessing rather than His curse? It was understood by the nation as a whole, that a people incapable of self-governing their private behavior according to natural law—God's law—could not exist as a representative republic, and would eventually descend into either anarchy or totalitarian rule.

The most perfect way to subvert and destroy a free nation of virtuous people would be to attack them within their institutions of learning and undermine the pre-eminent role of religion and morality-what George Washington called the "*indispensable supports*" of political prosperity. John Adams also warned of the danger of abandoning our virtue and morality when he said *"Our Constitution was made only for a moral and religious people. It is wholly inadequate to the government of any other."*

This is indeed what has happened to America, and it happened while I sat on the sidelines and watched. John Loeffler at Steel-on-Steel painted a perfect word picture of what must happen if America is to be redeemed from our apathy when he equated the opponents of freedom and liberty to a spy who is now so close to the goal that he now no longer cares whether he is seen for what he really is; he's making a stark-naked sprint for the end-zone, knowing that the only thing that can stop him now is if the people in the stands charge out on the field and tackle him. He's only a few steps from his goal, and if he can cross the line, nobody will be able to do anything to stop the consequences. Do we have virtue enough to do that?

Leaders Wanted: Statesmen Only Need Apply

A Statesman is a man or woman of virtue, wisdom, diplomacy, and courage who inspire greatness in others and move the cause of Liberty.
(from the Mission Statement of George Wythe University - www.gw.edu)

"Americans will have to once again make a distinction between a politician and a statesman. A politician is one who studies the art of what it takes to get elected... A statesman on the other hand is concerned with truth, its conviction and his faithful adherence to it, regardless of the consequences. Most importantly, a statesman will seriously consider the oath that binds him to a faithful loyalty to the Constitution at the state or federal level."
(Paul Jehle, Plymouth Rock Foundation)

"What the statesman is most anxious to produce is a certain moral character in his fellow citizens, namely a disposition to virtue and the performance of virtuous actions."
(Aristotle)

Leaders

Our government leaders swear an oath to support and defend the Constitution of the United States before they are allowed to exercise the powers of their offices. This oath automatically requires those office holders to act as a check on usurped or abused power among those within ANY branch of government. Why is it then, that when the Congress assumes powers for reserved by the Constitution to the states or the people, the President doesn't object with a defense of the Constitution and refuse to execute unlawful legislation? Or when the President creates Soviet-styled "czars" to violate the public rights, why doesn't the Congress speak up? Or when the court begins striking down the laws of the union states in violation of the public rights and in favor of "international norms" why don't the other two branches bring misdemeanor charges against those offending judges?

It appears that our leaders in government think that a non-intervention policy on another branch's behavior is more virtuous than executing the oath they took to support and defend the Constitution.

James Madison said in the Federalist Papers No. 51 that if men were angels, no government would be necessary, and that if angels were our governors, no Constitution would be necessary. Our Constitution IS necessary, however, and our public officials are proving to us the very reason this is so. The Constitution outlines the restricted powers WE THE PEOPLE gave to our governors. For our leaders to disobey them is to break the supreme law of the land, which is to be dealt with by impeachment and removal from office. I think the only way to effectively insure the reinstatement of our American form of law and government is to replace nearly every last congressman with one who will honor his oath.

AMERICAN DICTIONARY OF THE ENGLISH LANGUAGE – Noah Webster, 1828:

Common Law (Case Law)

"The unwritten law, the law that receives its binding force from immemorial usage and universal reception, in distinction from the written or statute law...that body of rules, principles, and customs which have been received from our ancestors, and by which courts have been governed in their judicial decisions.

"The evidence of this law is to be found in the reports of those decisions, and the records of the courts. Some of these rules may have originated in edicts or statutes which are now lost, or in the terms and conditions of particular grants or charters; but it is most probable that many of them originated in judicial decisions founded on natural justice and equity, or on local customs."

CONSTITUTION OF THE UNITED STATES, 7th Amendment: "In Suits at common law, where the value in controversy shall exceed twenty dollars, the right of trial by jury shall be preserved, and no fact tried by a jury, shall be otherwise re-examined in any Court of the United States, than according to the rules of the common law."

BLACK'S LAW DICTIONARY, Revised 4th Edition:

"Federal Common Law is a body of decisional law developed by the federal courts untrammeled by state court decisions."

"The Common Law may designate all that part of the positive law, juristic theory, and ancient custom of any state or nation, which is of general and universal application, thus marking off special local rules or customs."

Common Law

In the 2008 election cycle, the state leadership of the Constitution Party asked me to run for the 5th District seat of the US House of Representatives. During one of the candidate forums, while listening to the superior court judge segment, the candidates were asked what they thought about the doctrine of jury nullification. One of the answers in particular should make your hair stand up. One candidate explained that juries used to be instructed that they had the power to judge the law as well as the facts, but that we don't operate the courts and legal system under common law anymore; they are under statute law now, so judges have to tell juries how they must decide a verdict.

That one fact should explain, for Christians at least, why justice seems to be eluding this nation's people in many areas, and this is why—Common Law is historically in America. a practical extension of Natural Law into the arena of justice, which Nature's God is extremely interested in. The very idea of right and wrong are an extension of natural law into the moral compass of a people and a nation. I think the court prohibition of school prayer and the discouragement of religious traditions have had the exact effect they were intended to have. The judges who authored that ruling surely must understand what Ben Franklin meant when he said *"Only a virtuous people are capable of freedom. As nations become corrupt and vicious, they have more need of masters."*

Remove from the courts an affinity for natural law, prohibit the instruction of basic right and wrong in the schools, which is the basis for justice which flows from the common law, and presto!- you have a people who lack ability to self-govern and now have more need of masters. Wonder who'll want that job? Maybe someone who loves having power over his fellow men?

Declaration of Independence
Artist, John Trumbull

The Creed

If a known atheist entered your church, would you automatically consider him a member in good standing because he was occupying space on church property? Now ask the same question about any organization which has a creed and an oath affirming it. You won't be admitted to most organizations without agreeing to their mission statement.

The United States of America is no different. We have a creed, and just because someone is sucking air on American soil doesn't mean they are one of us. That requires an understanding of our supreme law- our common law- and an oath of allegiance to our principles. Our creed is contained in the Declaration of Independence- the national charter- the fundamental reason our fathers created this nation. In a nutshell, and without the beautifully soaring prose, our fathers claimed that this nation stood on the footing that our individual as well as national rights come from Almighty God; that our government exists merely to secure for us those rights; and if the government ever becomes destructive of that end, the people must alter or abolish it.

To our great shame and imminent peril, we have installed into the public trust leaders who no longer think it necessary to govern their performance by the principles of the Declaration of Independence or to obey the supreme law of the land- the Constitution. This doesn't mean the Constitution isn't working anymore, it means our political class needs to be completely replaced with those from the body of citizens who mean to keep their oaths to support and defend our American creed. I beg you to pray for America, that real Americans will provide an alternative for voters in all future elections, and that the fakers will be routed by Providence.

CONSTITUTION PARTY PLATFORM: Bring the Government Back Home

"The closer civil government is to the people, the more responsible, responsive, and accountable it is likely to be. The Constitution, itself, in Articles I through VI, enumerates the powers which may be exercised by the federal government. Of particular importance is Article I, Section 8 which delineates the authority of the Congress.

The federal government was clearly established as a government of limited authority. The Tenth Amendment to the Constitution specifically provides that: "*The powers not delegated to the United States by the Constitution, nor prohibited by it to the States, are reserved to the States respectively, or to the people.*"

Over time, the limitations of federal government power imposed by the Constitution have been substantially eroded. Preservation of constitutional government requires a restoration of the balance of authority between the federal government and the States as provided in the Constitution, itself, and as intended and construed by those who framed and ratified that document.

We pledge to be faithful to this constitutional requirement and to work methodically to restore to the States and to the people their rightful control over legislative, judicial, executive, and regulatory functions which are not Constitutionally delegated to the federal government.

We stand opposed to any regionalization of governments, at any level, which results in removal of decision-making powers from the people or those directly elected by the people."

Civil Authority and Scripture

It has been my experience that when the actions or decrees of the civil authorities are questioned, it is common for Christians to recite the Scripture in Romans 13:1-2, which admonishes us to obey the authorities. This is well and good, but we need to exercise some critical thinking in this regard.

If obeying the "authorities" is God's will, then it would be imperative to understand that in this nation under the rule of law, the supreme authority under which our civil authorities must operate is the US Constitution; these are the by-laws which define and restrain the powers delegated to our government officials. That being said, it naturally follows that government conduct, or orders which are not pursuant to the intent of the Declaration and US Constitution are illegitimate. You're right, Christian; the authorities must be obeyed, especially by our government servants. But we are at a point where our civil authorities don't really think they are required to obey the supreme authority.

There are 17 powers of Congress defined in the Constitution, a handful for the President, and the powers of the Supreme Court may be almost entirely extinguished by Congress. But the current reach of federal power into the affairs of the Union is now near saturation, mostly illegitimate, and we are in dire need of a couple hundred real Americans who are willing to postpone their businesses and recreation for a few years in order to restore our federal government to it's intended limited role in the life of the Union. Then our newly unemployed Congressmen would have time to use their CFL light bulbs to see clearly what actual authority WE THE PEOPLE gave them.

PREAMBLE TO THE CONSTITUTION PARTY PLATFORM:

We affirm the principles of inherent individual rights upon which these United States of America were founded:

- ★ That each individual is endowed by his Creator with certain unalienable rights; that among these are the rights to life, liberty, property and the pursuit of happiness;

- ★ That the freedom to own, use, exchange, control, protect, and freely dispose of property is a natural, necessary and inseparable extension of the individual's unalienable rights;

- ★ That the legitimate function of government is to secure these rights through the preservation of domestic tranquility, the maintenance of a strong national defense, and the promotion of equal justice for all;

- ★ That history makes clear that left unchecked, it is the nature of government to usurp the liberty of its citizens and eventually become a major violator of the people's rights; and

- ★ That, therefore, it is essential to bind government with the chains of the Constitution and carefully divide and jealously limit government powers to those assigned by the consent of the governed.

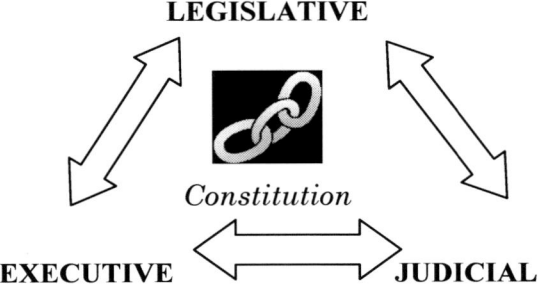

Principle vs. Politics

For many years, now, there has been a tremendous amount of attention paid to an almost endless list of policies and social engineering programs which our federal government has become infatuated with. The debates and arguments have an almost mesmerizing effect on us; so much so that I think that all this political gamesmanship is a pretty good vehicle to get us to forget the fact that much of what is being debated and argued has nothing to do with the Union states.

The *exclusive* legislative jurisdiction of the US Congress only affects Washington, D.C. and the territories owned by the US government, with the few exceptions enumerated in the Constitution. Most federal legislation is just hot air to a Union state exercising its sovereign authority.

For instance, federal gun control legislation is irrelevant in the Union states without a Constitutional amendment ratified by ¾ of the states granting that power. Same thing for any other act of Congress or federal statute which lays its hands on any power that hasn't been specifically delegated to the U.S. government by the Constitution.

So the 24/7 hand-wringing over the *cost* of a federal health care program, or *cost* of a bailout, is just politics, and reinforces the perception in minds that federal power *does* have authority in every sphere of life.

The same principles which *made* us free will *keep* us free; but we have stuck our noses so deeply into the minutia of politics that we have lost sight of the general principles that God used to bless this nation and make it, as Abraham Lincoln said, "*the last, best hope of mankind*".

CONSTITUTION PARTY PLATFORM: Congressional Reform

"The Senators and Representatives ... shall be bound by Oath or Affirmation, to support this Constitution". - US Constitution, Article 6, Clause 3

"With the advent of the 17th amendment, a vital check on Congress was removed. Since then, Congress has usurped power relatively unchecked, where today, very few members of Congress make it through a single session, without violating their oath of office to the Constitution...

It is time for the American people to renew effective supervision of their public servants, to restore right standards and to take back the government. Congress must once again be accountable to the people and obedient to the Constitution, repealing all laws that delegate legislative powers to regulatory agencies, bureaucracies, private organizations, the Federal Reserve Board, international agencies, the President, and the judiciary...

The U.S. Constitution, as originally framed in Article I, Section 3, provided for U.S. Senators to be elected by state legislators. This provided the states direct representation in the legislative branch so as to deter the usurpation of powers that are constitutionally reserved to the states or to the people. The Seventeenth Amendment (providing for direct, popular election of U.S. Senators) took away from state governments their Constitutional role of indirect participation in the federal legislative process...

If we are to see a return to the states those powers, programs, and sources of revenue that the federal government has unconstitutionally taken away, then it is also vital that we repeal the Seventeenth Amendment and return to state legislatures the function of electing the U.S. Senate. In so doing, this would return the U.S. Senate to being a body that represents the legislatures of the several states on the federal level and, thus, a tremendously vital part of the designed checks and balances of power that our Constitution originally provided."

Subversion

Just based on current facts before us, our nation's political leaders in elected office and both major parties have embraced policies and legislation subversive to our American form of law and government. Therefore, I think it profitable to visit the wisdom of our founding fathers regarding this kind of behavior.

Samuel Adams, regarding *"spreading the wealth around"* and centralized control of the economy, said the ideas *"are as visionary and impractical as those which vest all property in the Crown. They are arbitrary, despotic, and in our form of government, unconstitutional."* These charges could be aimed directly at our President and Congress today.

Thomas Jefferson wrote of a central government so strong that it borders on monarchy: *"These men have no right to office. If a monarchist be in office, anywhere, and it be known to the President, the oath he has taken to support the Constitution imperiously requires the instantaneous dismission of such officer; and I hold the President criminal if he permitted such to remain. To appoint a monarchist to conduct the affairs of a republic is like appointing an atheist to the priesthood."*

The situation in America today is socialism for WE THE PEOPLE and a political class who think they are monarchs rather than our agents; Congressmen openly insulting citizens exercising their 1st Amendment rights to redress? Congressmen taxing future generations without their consent? Presidents and judges approving of all this with their silence?

These will be our defining years in the eyes of our children and grandchildren, but if we DO nothing, we will COME to nothing. We need Americans in great numbers to join us.

CONSTITUTION OF THE UNITED STATES - Article 2, Section 4:

"The President, Vice President and all civil Officers of the United States, shall be removed from Office on Impeachment for, and Conviction of, Treason, Bribery, or other high Crimes and Misdemeanors."

AMERICAN DICTIONARY OF THE ENGLISH LANGUAGE – Noah Webster, 1828:

<u>High</u> means *"[a] great capital [offense]; committed against the king, sovereign, or state, as in high treason."*

<u>Crime</u> means *"an act which violates a law, divine or human; an act which violates a law of moral duty; an offense against the laws of right, prescribed by God or man, or against any rule of duty plainly implied in those laws."*

<u>Misdemeanor</u> means *"ill behavior; evil conduct; fault; mismanagement; minor wrongs against public rights."*

Andrew Johnson

William Clinton

Impeached Presidents

Crime and Rights

After first witnessing reliance on the Laws of Nature and Nature's God, the Declaration of Independence announces to the world that our rights come from God, and then explains that our government will be instituted in order to secure for us those rights. Our Constitution is the law within which our government must remain to secure them; otherwise *they are not secure*.

Natural Law informs that if we have a right, we also have a right and even a duty to protect and defend that right by whatever means necessary. This Constitutional, Natural Law defense of our rights extends to life, liberty, and property. Unless convicted of crime, rights may not be violated with impunity even by the State.

Our President and Congress are in the act of violating the rights of the American people by insisting that our right to defend our lives with medical care is only a privilege which they will dispense as they see fit; this is criminal. They have tried to do the same thing with the right to keep and bear arms and a multitude of other legislation.

Noah Webster was one of our founding fathers and wrote our first American dictionary. He knew what was meant by the Constitution's reference to "high crimes and misdemeanors"; misdemeanors are violations of the public rights or Natural Law, and in government are to be dealt with by impeachment and removal from office. Think these guys will impeach each other?

The lawless deeds of our federal government today beg God and the people for a replacement of our public servants by those with an American view of law and government. With the favor of Providence and your help it will be done.

CONSTITUTION PARTY PLATFORM: Character and Moral Conduct

John Adams, 2nd President and signer of the Declaration of Independence warned:

"Our Constitution was made only for a moral and religious people. It is wholly inadequate to the government of any other."

He also counseled:

"The people have a right, an indisputable, unalienable, indefeasible, divine right to that most dreaded and envied kind of knowledge - I mean of the character and conduct of their rulers."

Our very Constitution is threatened when we permit immoral conduct by our leaders. Public respect and esteem toward public officials has fallen to a shameful level. The Constitution Party finds that a cause of this national state of disgrace is the deterioration of personal character among government leaders, exacerbated by the lack of public outcry against immoral conduct by public office holders. Our party leaders and public officials must display exemplary qualities of honesty, integrity, reliability, moral uprightness, fidelity, prudence, temperance, justice, fortitude, self-restraint, courage, kindness, and compassion. If they cannot be trusted in private life, neither can they be trusted in public life.

It is imperative the members and nominated candidates representing the Constitution Party and its state affiliates recognize the importance of demonstrating good character in their own lives.

John Adams
Artist, John Trumbull

Religion and Morality

George Washington's Farewell Address is probably the most profound address ever given to this or any nation. In it he called religion and morality the "*indispensable supports*" of political prosperity.

Our founders defined religion to be "*the duty one owes to his Creator, and the manner of discharging it*". Noah Webster's dictionary calls religion and morality the duties of the first and second tables of the law. The tables he's talking about are the two tablets of the Ten Commandments; the first tablet dealing with our duties to God, and the second with our duties to our fellow man. He then cites Washington's Farewell Address as a reference of veracity.

Proverbs 28:4 tells us, "*They that forsake the law praise the wicked: but such as keep the law contend with them.*" Scripture's very plain here; our silence equals forsaking the law and proves by default that our religion and morality aren't worth a plug nickel. Our government officials and bureaucrats today are demanding that we allow and approve of behavior which we know in our spirits will bring God's judgment upon the entire nation. Our Declaration of Independence and U.S. Constitution are the products of the Laws of Nature and Nature's God; to sit silently while they are abused, defamed, forsaken and ignored is putting this nation in the path of God's wrath.

The first question a Congressman must ask is always "does this legislation decrease American freedom or individual liberty, or surpass Congress' limited Constitutional powers?" It's time to install new Congressmen who have the virtue to fulfill their oaths and contend for the Constitution. It's the morally responsible thing to do.

Congress

"I do solemnly swear (or affirm) that I will support and defend the Constitution of the United States against all enemies, foreign and domestic; that I will bear true faith and allegiance to the same; that I take this obligation freely, without any mental reservation or purpose of evasion; and that I will well and faithfully discharge the duties of the office on which I am about to enter: So help me God."

President

US Constitution, Article II, Section 1:

"I do solemnly swear (or affirm) that I will faithfully execute the office of President of the United States, and will to the best of my ability, preserve, protect, and defend the Constitution of the United States."

Supreme Court

According to Title 28, Chapter I, Part 453 of the United States Code, each Supreme Court Justice takes the following oath:

> *"I, [NAME], do solemnly swear (or affirm) that I will administer justice without respect to persons, and do equal right to the poor and to the rich, and that I will faithfully and impartially discharge and perform all the duties incumbent upon me as [TITLE] under the Constitution and laws of the United States. So help me God."*

The Oath of Office

Before a public official assumes the powers vested in that office, he is required to swear an oath to support and defend the US Constitution. An oath should not be taken lightly, as it is precious to Almighty God, and He will present it to the one who swore it when they inevitably meet at judgment day.

If your wife or child were being violated by someone, would you just argue that you don't agree with the method of violation? Or would that someone be picking his teeth up off the floor with his broken arm? I vote for picking the teeth up off the floor.

This is the circumstance of the Union states today. Those who inhabit the power centers of government today have become the violators, ignoring their oaths. First, we need to pray for them that they will see the error of their ways and repent of their oath-breaking. Next, we need to pray that any mischief circumventing our Constitution be confounded immediately. Third, pray that any official who refuses to honor his oath will lose all public support for his reelection or reappointment. Lastly, and most importantly, we need to pray fervently and regularly that men of virtue and honor will allow themselves to be drafted into public service as representatives and senators. We are in the situation we are in today because those whom God has called to fill those positions in government have not answered their calls.

Our nation is being violated, and we must begin seeking out those who will honor their oaths, and electively knock the political teeth out of those who are playing fast and lose with the Constitution.

Thomas Jefferson, Notes on Virginia, 1782: *"...it is usual for the jurors to decide the fact, and to refer the law arising on it to the decision of the judges. But this division of the subject lies with their discretion only. And if the question relate to any point of public liberty, or if it be one of those in which the judges may be suspected of bias, the jury undertake to decide both law and fact."*

Thomas Jefferson, letter to Thomas Paine, 1789: *"I consider [trial by jury] as the only anchor ever yet imagined by man, by which a government can be held to the principles of its constitution."*

United States Supreme Court, Georgia v. Brailsford, 1794: Chief Justice John Jay wrote: *"It is presumed, that juries are the best judges of facts; it is, on the other hand, presumed that courts are the best judges of law. But still both objects are within your power of decision... you [juries] have a right to take it upon yourselves to judge both, and to determine the law as well as the fact in controversy".*

District of Columbia Circuit Court of Appeals, United States v. Dougherty, 1972: *"[The jury has an] unreviewable and irreversible power...to acquit in disregard of the instructions on the law given by the trial judge...The pages of history shine on instances of the jury's exercise of its prerogative to disregard uncontradicted evidence and instructions of the judge; for example, acquittals under the fugitive slave law."*

Chief Justice of the Washington State Supreme Court, William C. Goodloe: Suggested that all judges give the following instruction to juries – *"You are instructed that this being a criminal case you are the exclusive judges of the evidence, the credibility of the witnesses and the weight to be given to their testimony, and you have a right also to determine the law in the case. The court does not intend to express any opinion concerning the weight of the evidence, but it is the duty of the court to advise you as to the law, and it is your duty to consider the instructions of the court; yet in your decision upon the merits of the case you have a right to determine for yourselves the law as well as the facts by which your verdict shall be governed."*

Jury Nullification

Since my commentary on Common Law, it has been asked why jury nullification matters. Say you are in the jury pool and being questioned for duty. Maybe the defendant didn't buy health insurance. Either the judge or prosecutor will ask you "will you apply the law even if you don't agree with it?" This question should require the immediate revocation of their license to practice law, because if you don't answer yes, you will be dismissed. Compare that to these jury instructions from the first jury trial before the U.S. Supreme Court: "...*both objects are within your power of decision. You have a right to take upon yourselves to judge of both, and to determine the law as well as the fact.*" That was in 1794. This is from U.S. v. Dougherty in 1972 – "*The jury has an unreviewable and un-reversible power...to acquit in disregard of the instructions on the law given by trial judge...*"

In other words, no American is bound to obey orders from his servant the judge on how to decide a verdict. The juror has the *right* and *duty* to decide whether the law which he is presently judging is just; in relation to the life, liberty and property of his fellow Americans and the defendant before him. That's why jury nullification matters. The judge's role in a trial is to ensure equal protection under the law, not to demand of a juror that he decide in favor of a law that he thinks obnoxious to our American creed.

The county Sheriff has this same nullification authority relating to federal laws, with the added bonus that he can arrest and jail those federal officers who are using federal laws to violate the public rights.

GEORGE WASHINGTON'S FAREWELL ADDRESS, 1796:
"Europe has a set of primary interests, which have to us none, or very remote relation. Hence, she must be engaged in frequent controversies, the causes of which are essentially foreign to our concerns. Hence, therefore, it must be unwise in us to implicate ourselves, by artificial ties, in the ordinary vicissitudes of her politics, or the ordinary combinations and collusions of her friendships or enmities. "Why forego the advantages of so peculiar a situation? Why quit our own to stand upon foreign ground? Why, by interweaving our destiny with that of any part of Europe, entangle our peace and prosperity in the toils of European ambition, rivalship, interest, humor, or caprice?"

THOMAS JEFFERSON, FIRST INAUGURAL ADDRESS, 1801: "I deem [one of] the essential principles of our government, and consequently [one] which ought to shape its administration,...peace, commerce, and honest friendship with all nations, entangling alliances with none."

JOHN QUINCY ADAMS, WASHINGTON D.C., 4 July 1821: "America has abstained from interference in the concerns of others, even when the conflict has been for principles to which she clings....She goes not abroad in search of monsters to destroy. She is the well-wisher to the freedom and independence of all. She is the champion and vindicator only of her own."

JAMES MONROE, MONROE DOCTRINE, 2 December 1823:
"In the wars of European powers in matters relating to themselves we have never taken any part, nor does it comport with our policy so to do....Our policy in regard to Europe...is, not to interfere in the internal concerns of any of its powers..."

Treaties and Sovereignty

In December of 2009, our President is expected to agree to a climate change treaty in Denmark which raises the possibility of American sovereignty being surrendered. This potential outcome is terrifying many, but I want to give you some hope that all is not lost if we simply obey the US Constitution.

Any treaties our President signs must afterwards be ratified by the U.S. Senate before it can become the law of the land. We The People, in our Constitution, delegated EXCLUSIVELY to the U.S. House, the sole authority to tax us. If any treaty contains provisions for *foreign governments* to lay what amounts to a tax on Americans, the President and all signatory Senators who signed it would be in breach of their oaths to support and defend the Constitution, but hey, what's new? James Madison addressed the difference between a constitution and a treaty, and said *"it would be a novel and dangerous doctrine that a legislature could change the constitution under which it held its existence."* In other words, the Constitution must be changed by We The People through the process of ratification by the union states, not by the use of treaties.

To apply a treaty as a vehicle for surrendering our national sovereignty is a violation of American rights guaranteed by our Constitution, and denominated there as a misdemeanor actionable by impeachment and removal from office. I don't think our Senate will ask for impeachment hearings for themselves if they sign this Denmark treaty, so make a list of all who do sign it, because you will have to impeach them yourself at the next election they participate in.

JAMES MADISON:
"With respect to the two words 'general welfare,' I have always regarded them as qualified by the detail of powers connected with them. To take them in a literal and unlimited sense would be a metamorphosis of the Constitution into a character which there is a host of proofs was not contemplated by its creators," and *"If Congress can do whatever in their discretion can be done by money, and will promote the General Welfare, the Government is no longer a limited one, possessing enumerated powers, but an indefinite one, subject to particular exceptions."*

THOMAS JEFFERSON, letter to Albert Gallatin, 16 June 1817: *"[O]ur tenet ever was, and, indeed, it is almost the only landmark which now divides the federalists from the republicans, that Congress has not unlimited powers to provide for the general welfare, but were to those specifically enumerated; and that, as it was never meant they should raise money for purposes which the enumeration did not place under their action; consequently, that the specification of powers is a limitation of the purposes for which they may raise money."*

CONSTITUTION PARTY PLATFORM: Welfare
The Declaration of Independence declares *"all men ... are endowed by their Creator with certain unalienable Rights ...That to secure these rights, Governments are instituted among Men ..."* The Preamble of the US Constitution shows how these rights are to be secured including *"provide for the common defense, promote the general Welfare".*

Two clear distinctions should be made here:

1. **Provide** implies actively and financially supporting, promote implies a more passive approach. For example, I'll **promote** that we put on a grand feast, but I want you to **provide it**!
2. General Welfare is <u>not</u> the same as individual Welfare. General Welfare would benefit the people generally; individual Welfare targets a certain segment of society to benefit, such as the poor.

Providing Individual Welfare is <u>not</u> authorized in the Constitution.

General Welfare

For a hundred and fifty years, the federal government operated on the understanding that it is vested with certain powers to provide for the *"general welfare"* of these united States, and that the meaning of *"general welfare"* is carefully defined in the Constitution. James Madison, the recognized "father of the Constitution" and Thomas Jefferson, the author of the Declaration of Independence, both stated that the intended purpose of the *"general welfare"* clause was to limit the power to tax, and thereby restrain unchecked growth and reach of federal power over the states and the people. Listen to just an excerpt from Madison's warning of this very thing in his speech to the first US Congress:

> *"If Congress can apply money indefinitely to the general welfare, and are the sole and supreme judges of the general welfare...everything from the highest object of State legislation, down to the most minute object of policy, would be thrown under the power of Congress..."*

Can you say CFL light bulb?

We know that our government is manned by two parties who are holding up their middle finger to our Constitution, and us. We know we have to revisit this founding principle which helped make us prosperous and free, but it cannot be done with the same people who have engineered our bankruptcy and decline. That will require an American view of law and government from the US Congress right on to the state legislatures who will ratify the amendment to make it so.

Scenes from the First American Revolution

Molly Pitcher

Nathan Hale Hanged by the British, 1776

Destruction at Boston Harbor

Paul Revere's Midnight Ride

The Birth of Old Glory

The Creator

It is a universally recognized phenomenon that children have a tendency to test or disobey their parents in order to be their own boss; to "get their way". The first recorded instance of this is found in the Biblical account of Adam and the entrance of sin and death into the world. Scripture refers to this as the sin nature which is inherent in mankind, and which cannot be conquered but through the avenue of being "born of the Spirit", as our Lord instructed in the Bible. The phenomenon does not end at the family, or at a particular age, however; it extends to governments and nations as well, and in America today we can see it in 3D. Our government is the child of We The People, and in the Constitution we laid out some very restrictive rules for it to follow. True to reality, this child is testing every inch of its boundaries in order to "be my own boss", and this child has now begun to abuse its parents with contemptuous disrespect and nearly unchecked power.

Our Founding Fathers stated in the Declaration of Independence that the reason we create government is to secure for us those rights which are given us by our Creator. Also in the Declaration is the dictate that should this government ever become destructive of those ends, it is both the right and the duty of the people to throw off that insolent government and replace it with one which will honor its duty to secure for us those rights which our Creator has endowed us with. I submit that the time for doing that very thing is now upon us with an urgency of critical proportions.

Randall Yearout

A Constitutionist's Proposal for Restoring the American Republic

There is an almost tangible restlessness in the American heart today. It is born of a sense that something needs to change; that something is wrong with the direction our government is going in relation to how we think things ought to be; that our peace and security as a people and a nation are in peril; and that if things don't change, there will be sorrow and regret, shame and poverty in our future. Indeed, there is a sense that it has already begun.

Democrats and Republicans have sensed this restlessness and made sweeping changes- in the wrong direction- away from common sense and our tried and true American form of constitutional law and government our founders gave us, and into the clutches of political and economic philosophies that spell doom and failure for our American experiment and therefore all of us; saddling us and our descendants with crushing debt - which alone can destroy our national independence, and surrendering our national sovereignty- and therefore our ability to control and decide our national destiny, to foreign interests who are increasingly proving themselves hostile to our values and priorities as a people and a nation. D and R policies are proving to be a disaster for America.

The tangible part of this American restlessness is almost unnamed because of its disguised presence. It is tangible not because WE are touching the thing, but rather because, and unknown to most, the thing is touching US in the form of statutes, regulations, and Acts of Congress which are being unconstitutionally (and therefore unlawfully) applied to the Union states and the American people. These are introduced by "penumbras and emanations" coming from the judiciary, codified by the legislative, and then administered by the executive. This entire process has the appearance of law because it takes place within the confines of the branches of government which have been delegated the authority to exercise great powers under the PUBLIC TRUST. This is why you say "they can't do that" every six months, but they do anyway, and then you stand there and feel helpless and insignificant. Our trust has been too complete, and now because of a lack of jealous guardianship of our Constitution by the American people, our national leaders are implementing plans which will impoverish and very possibly make us homeless on the continent our forefathers conquered.

America's moms and dads can't borrow and steal and spend themselves into peace and independence and prosperity, and our government, in spite of our leaders' assurances otherwise, cannot do it either. As a matter of fact, a government has less of a chance of doing so, because government by its very nature is capable only of either protecting or consuming the wealth that people create with their industry and ingenuity.

The Constitution Party thinks there is an American way to restore peace of mind to our people and prosperity to our nation, and it doesn't require borrowing, stealing, or spending by the federal government. It DOES involve moving in the direction of our founding fathers regarding a couple of very important principles which have been ignored and ridiculed by the political, academic and globalist elite of our day, whose view of this nation is as a power source to be used for their own self-aggrandizement; an economy to be milked for their own gratification. The whole lot of them wouldn't amount to a pimple on James Madison's butt.

Most Americans see these united States as our country, a very special place in the world which has been blessed by God with unparalleled success and favor; and because of that, needs to be preserved and operated as our fathers intended- under the rule of law; this is what has brought us peace and prosperity. America is not just an economy, it's our country; it's our home. And if we are to keep it a free, prosperous and peaceable home, we will have to make some changes which will necessarily restrain the unchecked growth and reach of federal power into the affairs of the people and the states. This absolutely MUST be done, because the only way government can grow is by consumption of our wealth, and our liberty. I probably don't need to tell you that both are becoming somewhat scarce.

So then, this is how I propose to accomplish the goal of rolling back and restraining the tendency of government to continually grow. If the proposal meets the approval of the American people, the Constitution Party should expect to see an increase in membership and support. Regardless of party affiliation, however, all supporters of restoring our republic are needed and welcome. Our motto, after all, is "principle over politics". It just makes sense to me that to expect the leadership and major contributors of the D's & R's to offer anything but opposition and treachery to any proposal which effectively dismantles the political/economic world which they have engineered and saddled us with would be unrealistic and probably an extremely frustrating waste of time and resources.

The proposal has several elements which must be passed by large majorities in both houses of Congress and the state legislatures, and we must understand that passage of these measures cannot even begin until a Congress committed to this work has been seated. The proposal must be accepted by the middle class and small business by margins large enough to ensure the election of representatives and Senators who are committed to them. They are:

1. A Constitutional Amendment to define the "general welfare" clause in its originally intended form.
2. A Constitutional Amendment to explicitly define the meaning of "income" to exclude the wages of labor, as per the original intent of the authors of the 16th Amendment.
3. Revoke the charter of the Federal Reserve to set monetary policy, and profit by charging for services which this nation can do for itself for nothing.
4. Begin the immediate reissuance of American currency in the form of gold and silver coin.
5. Encouragement of the states to educate their citizens and sheriffs of their last resort to check the power of bad laws by exercising their powers of nullification.
6. Restore the now extinct state check on federal power.

#1 - "General Welfare" clause

The ability of Congress and the Court to appropriate or rule on behalf of the *"general welfare"* of the Union must be restricted to the limits placed by the original intent of the general welfare clause and the enumerated powers of Congress. This will in the end have to be done by Constitutional Amendment. In order to accomplish this we will need to begin filling our federal and state House and Senate seats with those who will pledge to work for passage and ratification of an amendment to the US Constitution which will again bring the *"general welfare"* clause of the Article 1 powers of Congress back under the original intent of our founders.

Why? The supreme Court, in rulings for the last 70 years, has created a perception in the minds of Americans that Congress or the Court has authority to apply the term *"general welfare"* to anything they want to spend money on or to influence. And that perception has enabled our government in all three branches to abuse and violate our trust and our rights by taking more and more and more of the fruit of our labor (and now even the fruit of the labor of our descendants) to spend on projects and programs never delegated to their authority under the Constitution. This is the root of the tangible *"thing"* which is touching us all and giving us the feeling that something really needs to be fixed, if we only knew what *"it"* was. I assert that dealing with *"general welfare"* will fix it. Listen to James Madison, the recognized *"father of the Constitution"*, at the first United States Congress as he warns of perverting the *"general welfare"* clause: *"If Congress can apply money indefinitely to the general welfare, and are the sole and supreme judges of the general welfare, they may take the care of religion into their own hands; they may take into their own hands the education of children, establishing in like manner schools throughout the Union; they may undertake the regulation of all roads, other than post roads. In short, everything from the highest object of State legislation, down to the most minute object of policy, would be thrown under the power of Congress; for every object I have mentioned would admit the application of money, and might be called, if Congress pleased, provisions for the general welfare."*

Madison put his finger right on that *"sneaking hunch"* most of us have had as we've watched our government engage itself in things that made us think *"they can't do that! ... can they?"* If our government is to be limited in its power to reach into the affairs of the Union states and their individual citizens, it must be **constitutionally** prohibited from assigning the term *"general welfare"* to activities which are outside its specifically delegated responsibilities. The *"chains of the Constitution"* with which Jefferson intended to bind down the avarice and ambition of those in the federal government have at this point been proven by historical precedent to require strengthening, in order to prevent the apparently irresistible desire of men in power to tax and spend through the abuse of this clause. This recently perverted interpretation of the *"general welfare"* creates a grant of unlimited power instead of the founders' intended limitation on the power to tax. It also completely destroys the very idea of a limited federal government, and in the same stroke annihilates the sovereignty of the Union states.

Remember, whenever a government is either delegated a power or simply takes it from the rightful owner, it must also pay for the various agencies and employees and their overhead costs which are associated with administering that power. The federal government today is by far the largest employer in the country, employing itself in activities which were never intended by the founders or allowed by the Constitution; and our federal government is - without a doubt - the most budget-free zone in the world.

This measure will have the immediate effect of permanently halting earmarks, new entitlements, pork-barrel projects, and special-interest legislative favors being tacked onto spending bills. The result over several years will be the phasing out of the myriad executive branch agencies which have their fingers in almost every area of our lives. The services provided by these various bureaus and agencies, if still required by the Union states, may easily and with far more economy be continued by them individually.

This process will prove convulsive for some segments of the nation; mostly those in the employ of Uncle Sam in the Executive department agencies and their support industries, but the alternative is to not take this measure and be completely destroyed by the avarice, ambition, cowardice and ignorance of our current office-holders. When our government is

constitutionally restrained from taxing and spending for every conceivable project under the sun under the heading of *"general welfare"*, and limited only to those responsibilities which the Constitution allows, ALL of America will benefit. And our Congressmen will not be able to buy their jobs from us with promises to *"bring home the bacon"*. The bacon they promise us is our own money, confiscated by the government in order to pay for *"general welfare"* projects. In most cases, there's no reason for the *"bacon"* to go to Washington, DC in the first place, so we really don't need some politician to bring it back to us. How about the bacon staying in our pockets, and we'll decide what to do with it?

Now, with this measure dealing with the general welfare having been implemented, the effect will be a vastly smaller requirement for revenues, which brings us to the administrative function of government, related to the taxing power- the IRS.

2 - Income Tax

We must encourage passage and ratification of an amendment to prohibit application of the 16th Amendment *"income"* tax onto the personal labor, salaries, and property of the American people.

For the last 25% of this nation's history, the Congress has been employing a direct tax on our personal labor; what the Court has termed in years past as our *"most sacred and inviolable property"*. The tax on our personal labor began being collected at roughly the same time as the perversion of the *"general welfare"* clause was taking place. The executive branch, and its agent IRS, insist that the 16th Amendment authorizes the levying of taxes on incomes, and this is certainly true. But here is another redefinition of terms which has been hijacked from the common vocabulary, and applied to something unintended by the authors. The Congressional Record of the debates surrounding the formulation of the *"income"* tax amendment makes it clear that neither the country at large nor the Congress considered the *"wages"* a man received for his personal labor to be synonymous with *"income"*. This same understanding appears in the papers of record and the Courts. Not to belabor the point, but look at just two examples of this sentiment spanning forty years:

Senator Sherman in 1872) *"...Everyone must see that the consumption of the rich does not bear the same relation to the consumption of the poor as the income of the one compares with the wages of the other. ...Our party has ever contended that the burdens of the government should be at least partially shifted from the backs of the poor to those who can bear it; to divide them between the man who has nothing but his labor and the man who has incomes many times greater, derived from fortunes made by others;"* Cong. Rec. 4433 (1909).

Kentucky Governor A.E. Wilson in 1911) *"...The poor man or the man in moderate circumstances does not regard his wages or salary as an income..."*

"Income" was deemed to be the profits resulting from invested capital. Today, the collections from the misapplication of this tax accounts for over half of federal revenues. An American Congress obeying the originally intended limit on its taxing power within the *"general welfare"* powers of Congress would have no need for the vast amounts of taxes wrongly collected today from the wages of personal labor. This correction would provide an immediate 15 – 35% wage increase. It would save business at least the labor and expense of administering the paperwork and record-keeping required to meet the demands of this misapplied tax. The middle class would have the fruit of their labor to spend on what they will. And that would mean an economic stimulus which would NOT have to be borrowed from China, would NOT have to be paid back with interest, and would by all means create a higher standard of living for the entire middle class. IRS would be downsized and confined to its legitimate role of tax collection from its only 2 legitimate sources; 1) those entities existing at the government's pleasure (corporations) who are taxed by imposts, excises and duties, and 2) the profits, *"incomes"*, resulting from invested capital- in other words, *"income"* taxes.

Our goal is that the labor and lives of our descendants will never again be used as bargaining chips to collateralize unconstitutional, unconscionable, stupid, self-indulgent borrowing and spending such as we see today. We will have arrived at a proper understanding of federal taxing authority over personal labor and property when we have amended the 16th Amendment to indicate that *"income"* does not mean wages or salaries. This is very high on the Constitution Party's priority list, as you may have gathered by our **national toll-free telephone number – 1-800-2VETO-IRS.**

#3 - Federal Reserve

Part and parcel to the 16th Amendment was an Act of Congress which unconstitutionally delegated its authority to a private banking cartel called the Federal Reserve. The Act is operating upon the Union as if it had Constitutional authority, without all the messy inconvenience of having been ratified by ¾ of the states. This fact tells us that the Act is illegitimate outside the properties where the US government exercises *"exclusive legislative jurisdiction"*. We must extricate ourselves from this monstrosity and the various *"boom and bust"* cycles which it uses to fleece Americans of our wealth. I will support Rep. Ron Paul's **proposed bill to end the Fed, which brings us to proposal:**

#4 - Legal Tender

Restore gold and silver coin as the only legal tender in payment of debts. Article 1 Section 10 of the Constitution states that *"no state shall make anything but gold and silver coin a tender in payment of debt"*. This is intended as a protection against currency devaluation (inflation) caused by printing more paper bills than can be redeemed with the real currency. Legal tender is the medium of exchange which must be used for payment of debt if that is what the one who is owed the debt insists on. So if a debtor owes you $100, he may not present you with a bag of chicken gizzards or Federal Reserve notes and declare the debt paid in full, unless you consent to that exchange.

In 1920, an average blue-collar wage would provide about $20 a week; a one-ounce gold coin – the *"double eagle"*. That's about a thousand dollars a year; well below today's tax liability threshold. In today's economy, if your salary could be paid with the same ounce of gold, it will take twelve hundred Federal Reserve dollars to pay you. It may look like you are making a fairly large salary- 60k per year in paper money, but now you are in a 35% tax bracket. The government, by devaluing the currency, now has defrauded you of 35% of your earnings.

That gold coin would have purchased a very nice suit of clothes in 1920, and so would its corresponding gold or silver certificate – the paper money in that day which was redeemable in gold or silver coin from your bank. Today, that same $20 one-ounce gold coin will still purchase a fairly good suit. What kind of suit do you think that $20 Federal Reserve note will buy? About the same kind of suit that a bag of chicken gizzards will. This is how inflation of the paper money supply affects your standard of living. Apply this same (logic?) to a graduated tax code, and you will see the attraction paper money has to those in Congress or the Administration who need more and more tax revenues to pay for the expansion of their *"general welfare"* projects. As the paper money supply becomes worth less and less, you will need to be paid with more and more of it to sustain livable earnings, but the more you are paid, the higher tax bracket you move into. We will eventually all be in the highest tax bracket in spite of actually having a lower standard of living. Apparently those in control of this system think this is brilliant; for those who lack Christian virtue and morality, I suppose it is. I think its constructive fraud and can be remedied by a return to the Constitution's provisions for our national coinage. As a Constitutionist, I will work toward reinstating gold and silver as the base of our monetary system.

#5 - Nullification

Another important but overlooked *"tangible"* in the life of our republic is the conduct of our judicial proceedings in the matter of *"jury nullification"*, or *"jury lawlessness"*. The citizenry of America need to be reacquainted with their duty to their country and fellow citizens to exercise their own *"judicial review"* of the laws used to prosecute their neighbors and countrymen. The judges and bar of this nation have been refusing to inform jurors of their right to *"nullify"* bad laws by returning *"not guilty"* verdicts even if the defendant actually broke the particular law which he is being prosecuted under. Why is this important?

Say you are in the jury pool and being questioned for duty. Maybe the defendant is being prosecuted for not having health insurance. The judge will either tell you *"you must apply the law as I give it to you"* or maybe the prosecutor will ask you *"will you apply the law even if you don't agree with it?"* or something similar. This is a universal practice used to cleanse a jury of those citizens who can recognize an unconstitutional application of law, exposing a defendant to the injustice of having his rights and/or property violated by the government under color of law.

The jury is the last line of defense, short of armed resistance, against government using unjust laws to prosecute citizens. Listen to these jury instructions from the first jury trial before the US supreme Court: *"...both objects are within your power of decision. You have a right to take upon yourselves to judge of both, and to determine the law as well as the fact."* That was in 1794. This is from US v. Dougherty in 1972 – *"The jury has an unreviewable and un-reversible power...to acquit in disregard of the instructions on the law given by trial judge..."* In other words, no American is bound to obey orders from his servant the judge on how to decide a verdict. And no judge or prosecutor should be suffered who would excuse from duty those whose sense of justice will not allow them to apply a bad law, or misapply a good law, to one of their countrymen. The juror has the right and duty to decide whether the law which he is presently judging is just; in relation to the life, liberty and property of his fellow Americans and the defendant before him. That's why jury nullification matters. The judge's role in a trial is to ensure equal protection under the law, not to demand of a juror that he decide in favor of a law that he thinks obnoxious to our American creed.

The county Sheriff has this same nullification authority relating to federal laws, with the added bonus that he can arrest and jail those federal officers who are using federal laws to violate the public rights.

We will work to make sure that America knows that while juries are seated, they are judging the law as well as the facts.

#6 - State Sovereignty

State legislative impeachment advisory oversight of the federal Courts. I believe that the Union states must begin wielding the power necessary to keep the federal courts within at least a semblance of American jurisprudence. The rulings in recent years purportedly overturning state laws prohibiting homosexuality, non-denominational prayers in schools, curriculum selection in local schools, property rights such as the Kelo decision, environmental protection rulings, affirmative action, and on and on, are verifying a now commonly held belief among most Americans that our judges, as Thomas Jefferson said, *"are AS virtuous as the rest of us, not more so."* And their decisions need to be overseen by the combined state legislatures in order to protect the sovereignty of the Union and the States, and by extension, the freedoms and liberties of our citizens.

The independent judicial branch has been a blessing, for the most part, in the course of our American history; and for a great deal of our history, it has been acceptable and safe. But for several generations now, we have seen a judiciary which has set itself against the plain and simple principles which made us independent, strong, prosperous and free. This is scarcely remarkable, given the fact that most of our bar and bench is inhabited by graduates of Universities which actually profess a disdain for the Natural Law which our founding fathers held in such high esteem as to make of first prominence in our national charter, the Declaration of Independence. Natural Law is of course, the seed bed and strength of what our bar and bench is SUPPOSED to seek fervently – JUSTICE.

The judiciary opened the door to unrestrained federal power and reach into the affairs of the Union states and the people's lives when it ruled in 1936 that *"general welfare"* meant anything the government wanted it to mean. This *"interpretation"* virtually destroyed the concept of a **constitutionally** limited government (VERY bad behavior), and our US Congress should by all rights have impeached and removed from office the justices who so ruled, by virtue of the fact that a misdemeanor, a crime, had just been perpetrated by the judiciary. A misdemeanor is defined in the dictionary of our founders as a violation of the public rights, and in the Constitution high crimes and misdemeanors are punishable by impeachment and removal. By the time of this ruling, the states had already been 20 years without their own check on federal encroachment since passage of the 17th Amendment in 1913, when the selection of US Senators was taken away from the state legislatures and awarded to the general election of the people. But today, after almost 100 years, that state check on federal encroachment has yet to be replaced. I think it is time we reinstate a state check of the federal power before we are destroyed.

In fact, however, if the unlimited application of the *"general welfare"* clause is denied the Congress, as I have proposed in point #1, the state's check may not need to be employed against the Congress. It appears that the more dangerous department is the Judiciary, whose rulings have historically been the watershed which has unleashed the types of legislation which has, for all practical purposes, made administrative subdivisions of our (formerly) sovereign Union states. It is out and out breach of oath that our US Representatives and Senators have been unwilling to take the initiative to check the Judiciary, even in the face of the most treacherous behavior, but as I have said earlier, this is the government the two major parties and their major contributors want, or it wouldn't exist as it does today.

I think it profitable here to repeat James Madison again regarding our responsibility to preserve our liberty as Americans:

"...it is proper to take alarm at the first experiment of our liberties. We hold this prudent jealousy to be the first duty of citizens and one of the noblest characteristics of the late Revolution. The freemen of America did not wait till usurped power had strengthened itself by exercise and entangled the question in precedents. They saw all the consequences in the principle, and they avoided the consequences by denying the principle. We revere this lesson too much, soon to forget it."

Our federal judiciary has too often been the first usurper in our national life, and following its lead, the general government has definitely *"strengthened itself by exercise and entangled the question in precedent"*. From Madison's advice, I believe the case can and should be made that the body closest to the people should be the initiators of impeachment proceedings against judges who have lost sight of our American form of law and government.

I propose that the state legislatures jointly monitor the rulings of federal courts for the purpose of advising their US Representatives and Senators of the propriety of instituting impeachment proceedings against members of the Judiciary when rulings are engaged which have the effect of violating the public rights or usurping state sovereignty.

It is as true today as in the colonial times when Thomas Paine wrote that *"Perhaps the sentiments contained in [these] ... pages are not yet sufficiently fashionable to procure them general favor; a long habit of not thinking a thing wrong gives it a superficial appearance of being right, and raises at first a formidable outcry in defense of custom."* There is a difference between our day and the colonial times, in the minds of the American public as to whether this needs to be done, however; I think America at large KNOWS this needs to be done, and we are those to whom the duty has fallen. We must do this.

In closing, want you to be aware of my unshakable belief that a Constitution honoring, oath honoring lawmaker cannot in good conscience work on legislation which has either the immediate or distant effect of engineering the decline of American freedom and the wholesale loss of individual liberty. Any legislator who is installed as your representative or senator should vote no, no, and no on anything which had that effect. It is necessary to do as Madison said and see the consequences in the principles being considered in legislation, and deny any principles which effectively ignore the supreme law of the land – the US Constitution. A waiting period would be necessary until my countrymen sent enough more representatives and senators to make an American congress again, in which case work could begin on the measures I just presented to you. As I said, to think the restoration of the Republic could be accomplished with the same congressmen who have been responsible for the engineering of American decline and stripping of our liberties would be insane. Find those who believe like you, send them to Washington.

Randall Yearout

About the Constitution Party

THE MISSION STATEMENT: *The mission of the Constitution Party is to secure the blessings of liberty to ourselves and our posterity through the election, at all levels of government, of Constitution Party candidates who will uphold the principles of the Declaration of Independence and the Constitution of the United States. It is our goal to limit the federal government to its delegated, enumerated, Constitutional functions and to restore American jurisprudence to its original Biblical common-law foundations.*

THE SEVEN PRINCIPLES:
- ★ Life - For all human beings, from conception to natural death.
- ★ Liberty - Freedom of conscience and actions for the self-governed individual.
- ★ Family - One husband and one wife with their children as divinely instituted.
- ★ Property - Each individual's right to own and steward personal property without government burden.
- ★ Constitution and Bill of Rights - Interpreted according to the actual intent of the Founding Fathers.
- ★ States' Rights - Everything not specifically delegated by the Constitution to the federal government is reserved for the state and local jurisdictions.
- ★ American Sovereignty - American government committed to the protection of the borders, trade, and common defense of Americans, and not entangled in foreign alliances.

A FEW OF THE ISSUES:
- Stop wasting trillions of dollars on unconstitutional programs
- Impeach activist judges who call their unconstitutional rulings law
- Keep all that you earn, as the income tax is replaced with a revenue tariff
- Defend the God ordained institution of marriage – one man, one woman
- Stop the exporting of American jobs
- Secure our borders – stop the illegal immigration invasion – reject amnesty

- Restore and preserve the right to keep and bear arms against any and all infringement
- Defend the property rights of Americans
- End Federal Subsidies for and Control of Education and Welfare
- Restore National Sovereignty, including Withdrawal from the U. N.

A HISTORY OF THE CONSTITUTION PARTY:

1992 - A coalition of independent state parties united to form the U.S. Taxpayers Party. The party's founder, Howard Phillips, was on the ballot in 21 states as its first presidential candidate.

1995 through 1999 – The Constitution Party is Party recognized by Federal Election Commission as a national party bringing the number of recognized parties to 5. Ballot access achieved in 39 states for the 1996 elections, representing over 80% of the Electoral College votes available.

1999 - Name changed to "Constitution Party" by delegates at the National Convention to better reflect the party's primary focus of returning government to the U.S. Constitution's provisions and limitations.

2000 & 2004 - The party achieved ballot access in 41 and 36 states respectively. Though the party was on fewer state ballots in 2004, the vote tally increased by 40% compared to the 2000 elections while other 'alternative' parties lost ground or barely matched their 2000 vote totals.

MOTTO: "Principles Over Politics"

CONSTITUTION PARTY OF WASHINGTON: www.constitutionpartyofwa.com
NATIONAL CONSTITUTION PARTY: www.constitutionparty.com